AR-15 Rifle Builder's Manual

An Illustrated, Step-by-Step Guide to Assembling the AR-15 Rifle

by Rob Reaser

AR-15 Rifle Builder's Manual
An Illustrated, Step-by-Step Guide to Assembling the AR-15 Rifle

© 2016 by Rob Reaser

published by RBC

All rights reserved. No part of this book may be reproduced or transmitted in any form by any means, electronic or mechanical or otherwise, without the prior written permission of the publisher.

All images are copyright by the author.

All persons, product names, trademarks and copyright materials identified or presented in this book are used in an editorial fashion only and with no intention of infringement of the trademark or copyright. No such use, or the use of any trade name, is intended to convey endorsement or other affiliation with this book.

Cover design and book production by RBC

FORWARD

The AR-15 style rifle is arguably the most popular firearm in the U.S. This is due, largely, to its unique ability to serve a broad range of sporting applications—from recreational and competitive shooting to hunting—as well as personal defense applications. In addition to its wide application, the rifle's popularity can also be credited to its do-it-yourself, customizable nature. The remarkable growth of aftermarket manufacturers who make replacement and upgraded components for the AR-platform rifles has further helped to make this firearm the cornerstone of the "black rifle" industry.

To be clear, though, and to give credit where it is due, there is only one true AR-15 rifle, and that is any rifle so-designated by Colt's Manufacturing Company, LLC. Colt is the registered owner of the AR-15 trademark, and all self-loading, intermediate-cartridge, magazine-fed, air-cooled, gas impingement system light rifles based on the Eugene Stoner/Armalite Rifle design that are not designated by Colt as an AR-15 are actually clones or modified clones of the true AR-15. That said, and much to the chagrin of Colt, "AR" and "AR-15" have devolved into colloquialisms referring to most civilian semi-automatic rifles based on the U.S. military's ubiquitous M4/M16-platform weapons.

While this book acknowledges the trademark rights of Colt's Manufacturing Company, LLC with regard to the AR-15 trademark, to minimize overburdened language or potential confusion to the reader, the terms AR or AR-15 are used here to imply "AR-15 style" firearms and components and not the actual trademarked "AR" or "AR-15" properties owned by Colt's Manufacturing Company, LLC.

One of the benefits of the large aftermarket AR parts industry is the ability for firearms enthusiasts to not only build their own rifle from start to finish, but also to customize their rifles to best suit their intended use—be that sport shooting, hunting, competition, or personal defense. Although there are many avenues to building an AR-style rifle, the fundamental assembly processes are common to all. For this reason, this book was developed to illustrate the detailed, step-by-step process of building the basic MILSPEC-style AR rifle. With this solid understanding of AR components and their assembly, the reader will have the knowledge base to customize his or her rifle—whether that be installing a premium trigger group, low-profile gas block and free-float handguard, different grips and buttstocks, or any number of modifications made available through the aftermarket.

IMPORTANT NOTICE I

This book was developed to illustrate the assembly process of an AR-15 style rifle. One should assemble or work on a firearm only if:

1) they possess the proper skills and tools to do so, and

2) they have thoroughly read and understand the assembly processes prior to working on a rifle.

The author and publisher will not be held responsible for accidents resulting from the improper use of the information in this book.

IMPORTANT NOTICE II

This book does not include a ready-made parts list for assembling an AR-15 style rifle because of the variations available in the market. There is, however, a detailed listing of all assembly components and required tools at the beginning of each section of this book. The reader can use these as a guide for acquiring the necessary components to build their rifle. The author recommends one-stop shopping from a source such as Brownells or Midway USA.

IMPORTANT NOTICE III

The lower receiver is the ATF-controlled item of an AR-15 style rifle. Purchase of a stripped lower receiver is treated like any other firearms acquisition. It must be purchased through a Federal Firearm License (FFL) dealer and the buyer must complete Form 4473 and pass the requisite background check before taking possession of a receiver.

AR-15 Rifle Builder's Manual

AR-15 Rifle Builder's Manual

TABLE OF CONTENTS

SECTION I: AR-15 IDENTIFICATION & OVERVIEW 1
Identification
General Specifications

SECTION II: LOWER RECEIVER GROUP 3
Lower Receiver Components 3
Lower Receiver Assembly Tools 4
Magazine Catch Assembly 4
Bolt Catch Assembly 5
Pivot Pin Assembly 8
How the AR Trigger Works 10
Trigger Group Assembly 11
Trigger Group Preliminary Function Check 15
Trigger Guard Assembly 17
Pistol Grip Assembly 18
Buttstock Assembly 20

SECTION III: UPPER RECEIVER GROUP 27
Headspacing 27
Bolt Carrier Group
    Bolt Carrier Group Components 30
    Bolt Carrier Group Assembly Tools 30
    Firing Pin Protrusion Check 30
    Bolt Carrier Group Assembly 31
Upper Receiver Group Components 37
Upper Receiver Assembly Tools 37
Ejection Port Cover Assembly 38
Forward Assist Assembly 39
Front Sight Base/Gas Tube Assembly 41
Barrel Assembly 43
Flash Hider Assembly 47
Charging Handle & Bolt Carrier Group Installation 48
Carry Handle/Rear Sight Assembly 49
Handguard Installation 50

SECTION IV: UPPER/LOWER RECEIVER ASSEMBLY & FUNCTION CHECK 51
Upper & Lower Receiver Group Assembly 51
Function Check 51

SECTION V: AR-15 OPERATION 53
Magazine Loading 53
Loading and Discharging 54
AR-15 Cycle of Operation 55
Unloading and Making Safe 56
Zeroing and Marksmanship 58

SECTION VI: SERVICE & LUBRICATION 59
Rifle Cleaning and Lubrication 59
Magazine Service 62

SECTION VII: TROUBLESHOOTING 63

SECTION I – AR-15 IDENTIFICATION & OVERVIEW

IDENTIFICATION

TYPICAL AR-15 SPECIFICATIONS

Chamber: 5.56x45mm NATO
Barrel length: 16 inches
Action: Semi-automatic, direct impingement gas system/rotating bolt
Magazine: STANAG-style, 30 round capacity
Muzzle velocity: 3,100-3,200 fps

SECTION II – LOWER RECEIVER GROUP

LOWER RECEIVER COMPONENTS

Trigger group

1) disconnect, 2) disconnect spring, 3) trigger spring, 4) trigger, 5) trigger pin, 6) hammer, 7) hammer spring, 8) hammer pin

Magazine catch assembly

1) magazine release button, 2) magazine release button spring, 3) magazine catch

Fire control selector assembly

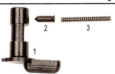

1) fire control selector, 2) fire control selector detent, 3) fire control selector detent spring

Pivot and takedown pin assemblies

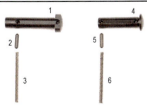

1) receiver pivot pin, 2) receiver pivot detent pin, 3) receiver pivot detent spring, 4) receiver takedown pin, 5) receiver takedown detent pin, 6) receiver takedown detent spring

Bolt catch assembly

1) bolt catch, 2) bolt catch pin, 3) bolt catch plunger, 4) bolt catch spring

Trigger guard assembly

1) trigger guard, 2) trigger guard pin

Pistol grip assembly

1) pistol grip, 2) pistol grip lock washer, 3) pistol grip screw

Buttstock assembly

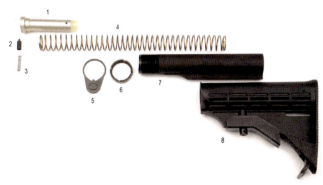

1) buffer, 2) buffer retainer, 3) buffer retainer spring, 4) action spring, 5) receiver end plate, 6) receiver extension nut, 7) receiver extension, 8) buttstock

Lower receiver

LOWER RECEIVER ASSEMBLY TOOLS

1) lubricant, 2) LocTite, 3) masking tape, 4) torque wrench - ft/lbs, 5) large punch, 6) anti-seize lubricant, 7) playing cards, 8) roll pin punches, 9) AR buttstock tool, 10) hex wrench, 11) hammer

MAGAZINE CATCH ASSEMBLY

1 Lightly lubricate the magazine catch shaft and threads.

2 Insert the magazine catch into the lower receiver.

3 Install the magazine release button spring over the magazine catch shaft.

4 Screw the magazine release button onto the magazine catch shaft.

5 Once the magazine release button is sufficiently threaded onto the magazine catch shaft, depress the release button against the receiver and rotate the magazine catch.

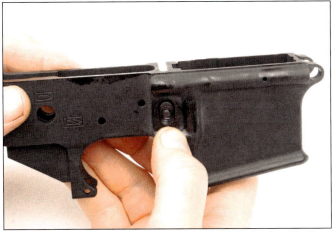

6 Tighten until the magazine catch shaft is flush with the magazine release button, as shown.

BOLT CATCH ASSEMBLY

7 When properly installed, the magazine catch should clear the magazine well when the magazine release button is depressed, allowing the magazine to fall out of the well.

1 Apply masking tape to the left side of the receiver, as shown, to prevent scratching or marring the receiver surface.

2 Lightly lubricate the bolt catch roll pin.

3 Use a suitable-sized roll pin punch and hammer to tap the bolt catch roll pin into the receiver bolt catch boss. NOTE: Only tap the roll pin until its end is flush with the inside of the receiver boss.

AR-15 Rifle Builder's Manual

4 The bolt catch roll pin correctly installed in the receiver bolt catch boss.

5 Lightly lubricate the bolt catch spring.

6 Insert the bolt catch spring into the receiver bolt catch hole.

7 Lightly lubricate the bolt catch plunger.

8 Insert the bolt catch plunger into the end of the bolt catch spring, as shown.

9 Depress the bolt catch plunger into the receiver bolt catch hole. The plunger will need to be aligned in the receiver bolt catch hole in order to properly install the bolt catch.

10 Lightly lubricate the bolt catch.

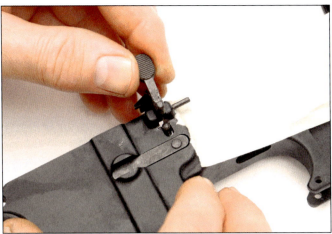
11 Insert the bolt catch between the receiver bolt catch bosses, as shown.

12 Align the bolt catch roll pin hole with the roll pin and push down to depress the bolt catch plunger.

13 With the bolt catch roll pin hole properly aligned with the bolt catch roll pin, use a hammer to tap the roll pin through the bolt catch and into the opposite receiver bolt catch boss.

14 It may be necessary to use a roll pin punch to seat the bolt catch roll pin.

15 When properly installed, the bolt catch roll pin should be flush or slightly recessed in the receiver bolt catch bosses, as shown.

AR-15 Rifle Builder's Manual

PIVOT PIN ASSEMBLY

1 Lightly lubricate the receiver pivot detent spring.

16 Test the bolt catch function to ensure there is no binding when you depress and release the bolt catch, and that the spring and plunger are working properly and smoothly.

2 Install the spring into the front of the receiver, as shown.

3 Lightly lubricate the receiver pivot detent pin.

4 Insert the receiver pivot detent pin into the receiver until it stays in position.

5 Lightly lubricate the pivot pin.

6 Align the pivot pin so that the detent groove is facing the detent pin.

7 Place the pivot pin against the detent pin, as shown.

8 (NOTE: The pivot pin installs under spring pressure, so be careful not to let the pivot pin slip sideways during the following step. Failure to maintain control of the assembly can result in the spring and detent pin ejecting from the receiver.) Push the pivot pin against the detent pin until the pivot pin is aligned with the pivot pin hole in the receiver.

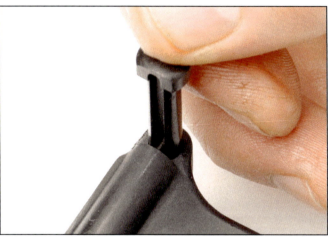
9 Push in on the pivot pin to seat it in the receiver. When properly installed, you will hear and feel the detent pin seating in the pivot pin detent groove.

10 The pivot pin, if properly installed, should easily slide through both of the receiver's pivot pin holes.

11 Pull the receiver pin out. When properly installed, the detent pin should secure the pivot pin in the receiver when the pivot pin is pulled outward, as shown.

HOW THE AR TRIGGER WORKS

The workings of an AR trigger are a mystery to many. That is unfortunate, as this knowledge is useful not only in terms of diagnosing mechanical problems, but also in refining one's shooting technique, and when installing aftermarket triggers. The following provides a visual overview of how the trigger system works.

2 This shows the hammer and trigger positions after the trigger has been pulled rearward. As the trigger pivots on the trigger pin, the sear engagement surface slides off the hammer's cocking searation, releasing the hammer to strike the firing pin.

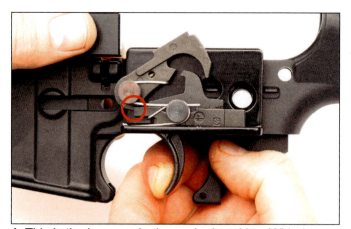

1 This is the hammer in the cocked position. With the fire control lever (not shown) in the FIRE position, the hammer will release when the trigger is pulled rearward. Notice how the hammer spring legs are positioned across the top of the trigger spring coil. When correctly installed, the hammer is under considerable and constant spring tension and wants to move forward at all times. What prevents the hammer from moving forward (toward the firing pin) when in the cocked position is the hammer's cocking searation and the trigger's sear engagement surface. These are shown within the red circle. The trigger spring tension (keeping the trigger forward) and the hammer spring tension (keeping the hammer's cocking searation pushed against the trigger's sear engagement surface) keep the hammer and trigger cocked. When the fire control selector (not shown) is in the SAFE position, the trigger cannot pivot on the trigger pin and subsequently disengage from the hammer cocking searation.

3 After the cartridge fires, gas pushes the bolt carrier rearward, which also pushes the hammer rearward, as shown. As the hammer travels backward and down, it is slowed by the disconnect.

4 The disconnect's sear engagement surface now captures the hammer and prevents it from traveling forward (red circle). All of this takes place while the trigger is still in its rearward position. In this position, a semi-automatic rifle cannot be fired again until the trigger group is "reset."

5 The trigger is reset when it is allowed to move forward. When this happens, the disconnect "disconnects" from the hammer. The hammer moves forward slightly and is immediately captured by the trigger's sear engagement surface. The trigger group is once again in the cocked position and the rifle is ready to fire.

TRIGGER GROUP ASSEMBLY

1 Lightly lubricate the hammer pin bosses as shown.

2 Install the hammer spring onto the hammer in the orientation shown.

3 The hammer spring correctly installed.

4 Lightly lubricate the trigger, as shown.

5 Install the trigger spring onto the trigger in the orientation shown.

6 The trigger spring correctly installed.

7 Lightly lubricate the disconnect spring.

8 Install the disconnect spring into its position in the trigger with the wide end of the coil oriented down into the spring seat, as shown.

9 The disconnect spring in place.

10 Install the disconnect onto the trigger in the orientation shown.

11 Lightly lubricate the trigger pin.

12 Install the trigger and disconnect assembly into the receiver, as shown. Note how the legs of the trigger spring lay across the bottom of the receiver.

13 Push/pull on the trigger and disconnect assembly until the trigger pin holes align with the receiver's trigger pin holes. Note that the assembly is under spring tension for this operation.

14 While maintaining trigger alignment, orient the trigger pin so that the pin grooves are on the fire control (safety selector) side of the receiver, as shown. Next, insert the trigger pin through the receiver and trigger.

AR-15 Rifle Builder's Manual

15 When properly installed, the ends of the trigger pin should be flush with the sides of the receiver.

16 Pull back and let up on the trigger to ensure it is correctly installed and working properly.

17 Lightly lubricate the fire control selector.

18 Insert the fire control selector into the receiver, as shown.

19 Lightly lubricate the hammer pin.

20 Insert the hammer into the receiver, as shown. Note the orientation of the hammer spring legs. These will ride on top of the trigger assembly. Like the trigger assembly, the hammer assembly must be installed while under spring tension; therefore, it is necessary to ensure the spring legs are in their proper position and that you maintain control of the assembly while installing the hammer pin.

21 Opposite view of the hammer spring laying atop the trigger assembly (arrow).

22 Push down on the hammer assembly until the hammer pin holes align with the receiver's hammer pin holes. Note that the assembly is under spring tension for this operation.

23 While maintaining hammer alignment, orient the hammer pin so that the pin grooves are on the fire control (safety selector) side of the receiver, as shown. With the holes aligned, insert the hammer pin through the receiver and hammer.

24 You can use a hammer to tap the hammer pin in place.

TRIGGER GROUP PRELIMINARY FUNCTION CHECK

25 When properly installed, the ends of the hammer pin should be flush with the sides of the receiver.

1 To ensure that the trigger group is correctly installed and functioning, perform a preliminary function check. Begin by pulling the hammer back, making sure it engages the trigger and remains in the cocked position. NOTE: Be sure to maintain control of the hammer throughout the function check, and do not allow the hammer to release and strike the receiver, as this could damage the receiver.

2 Test the trigger release by placing your thumb in front of the hammer, as shown, and pulling back on the trigger. If functioning properly, the hammer will fall forward.

3 With the hammer in the forward position, keep the trigger pulled back.

4 Keeping the trigger in the rearmost position, push the hammer all the way back and down until it engages the disconnect and can move no farther.

5 Still keeping the trigger in the rearmost position, let off the hammer.

6 Slowly let off the trigger. If the trigger group is functioning properly, you will feel and hear an audible click as the trigger resets. The hammer will move up slightly as it engages the sear, and will remain in the cocked position. If the trigger group did not perform as described, diagnose and correct the problem before moving on. Disassembly and reassembly of the trigger group may be required to correct the problem and ensure that all springs and components are in their proper position.

TRIGGER GUARD ASSEMBLY

1 The receiver's trigger guard tangs must have a flat support when installing the trigger guard roll pin, otherwise, the tangs may break and thus destroy the receiver when the roll pin is tapped into place. A simple way to provide the necessary support is to place the receiver on a flat surface. Next, stack an appropriate amount of playing cards beneath the bottom tang. This will ensure adequate support during the trigger guard installation.

2 The front of the trigger guard has a plunger that seats into the hole in the right side trigger guard tang.

3 Position the front of the trigger guard between the trigger guard tangs, depressing the plunger as you slide it into the tang.

4 The front of the trigger guard is correctly installed when the plunger snaps into place.

5 Position the back of the trigger guard between the rear tangs, aligning the trigger guard roll pin channel with the holes in the tangs.

6 Lightly lubricate the trigger guard roll pin.

AR-15 Rifle Builder's Manual

7 Start the roll pin into the tang by gently tapping it into place.

8 Use a roll pin punch to finish tapping the roll pin into place.

9 The correctly installed roll pin should be flush with the sides of the tangs.

PISTOL GRIP ASSEMBLY

1 Use an alcohol-based solvent to wipe clean the pistol grip screw threads.

2 Lightly lubricate the fire control selector detent.

3 Turn the receiver upside down and install the fire control selector detent into the receiver fire control selector detent and spring channel, as shown.

4 Lightly lubricate the fire control detent spring.

5 Insert the fire control detent spring into the pistol grip's spring channel, as shown.

6 Place the pistol grip screw (with the lock washer installed) onto an Allen wrench and insert it into the pistol grip.

7 Apply a small bead of Loctite 242 onto the end of the pistol grip screw.

8 Align the pistol grip with the receiver, as shown, being careful not to allow the fire control detent to fall out of the receiver. The fire control detent spring must start into its receiver channel.

9 Once everything is properly aligned, tighten the pistol grip screw snug into the receiver to complete the installation.

BUTTSTOCK ASSEMBLY

10 Ensure the fire control selector is working properly by moving the selector between the FIRE and SAFE positions. The selector should snap into and remain in each position. Test the selector function by cocking the hammer and pulling the trigger with the fire control selector in both the FIRE and SAFE positions (do not let the hammer fall against the receiver!). The trigger should not pull rearward and the hammer should not fall when the fire control selector is in the SAFE position. The trigger should pull rearward and the hammer should fall when the fire control selector is in the FIRE position.

1 Wipe clean the receiver extension threads with an alcohol-based solvent.

2 Wipe clean the receiver extension nut with an alcohol-based solvent.

3 Thread the receiver extension nut onto the receiver extension with the slots oriented toward the receiver extension, as shown.

4 Install the receiver end plate onto the receiver extension. The receiver end plate is keyed to the slot in the bottom of the receiver extension. Install the receiver end plate with the dimple oriented away from the receiver extension, as shown.

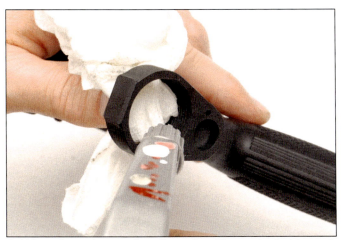

5 Wipe clean the receiver threads with an alcohol-based solvent.

6 Lightly lubricate the receiver takedown pin.

7 Install the receiver takedown pin into the receiver with the detent groove oriented toward the back of the receiver, as shown.

8 Lightly lubricate the receiver takedown detent pin.

9 Insert the receiver takedown detent pin into the takedown detent pin and spring channel at the back of the receiver.

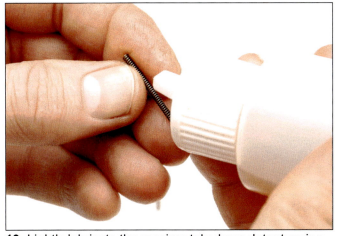

10 Lightly lubricate the receiver takedown detent spring.

11 Insert the receiver takedown detent spring into the takedown detent pin and spring channel at the back of the receiver.

12 Lightly lubricate the buffer retainer spring.

13 Insert the buffer retainer spring into the receiver, as shown.

14 Lightly lubricate the buffer retainer.

15 Insert the buffer retainer into the receiver, as shown. The buffer retainer sits on top of the buffer retainer spring.

16 Apply a light coating of anti-seize lubricant to the receiver threads.

17 Begin threading the receiver extension into the receiver.

18 When the end of the receiver extension reaches the buffer retainer, depress the buffer retainer until only the tip of the retainer protrudes above the receiver.

19 Continue to thread the receiver extension into the receiver until the end of the receiver extension is over the shoulder of the buffer retainer, as shown. When properly installed, the buffer retainer should be fully captured (held in place) by the receiver extension. Push down and let up on the buffer retainer. It should move up and down in the receiver without binding, yet remain secured by the receiver extension.

20 Use a small flathead screwdriver or similar tool to align/straighten the receiver takedown detent spring and simultaneously seat the spring into the receiver by pushing the receiver end plate against the back of the receiver.

21 While holding the receiver end plate in its correct position, apply a small bead of Loctite 242 to the exposed receiver extension threads.

22 Using your fingers, thread the receiver extension nut until it is snug against the back of the receiver end plate.

23 Position the AR buttstock wrench onto the receiver extension nut. The wrench will align with the slots in the nut.

24 Install a torque wrench onto the buttstock wrench and tighten the receiver extension nut to between 35 and 39 ft-lbs.

25 To ensure the receiver extension nut does not rotate loose, the nut should be staked to the receiver end plate. Do this by aligning the tip of a punch with one of the staking slots in the nut and striking the edge of the end plate enough to raise a burr. This burr will protrude into the extension nut slot enough to prevent the nut from rotating loose.

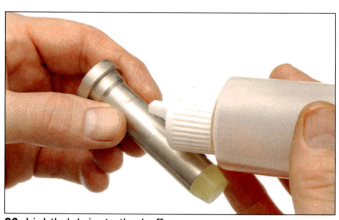

26 Lightly lubricate the buffer.

27 Lightly lubricate the action spring.

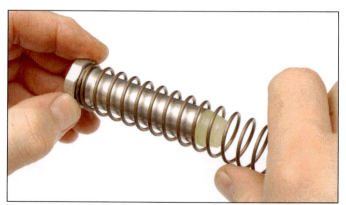

28 Insert the buffer into the end of the action spring, making sure that the spring is seated fully against the buffer shoulder.

29 Insert the buffer/action spring assembly into the receiver extension, as shown.

30 Depress the buffer retainer into the receiver to allow the buffer to slide fully into the receiver extension, then release the buffer retainer. The buffer retainer will keep the buffer/action spring assembly seated inside the receiver extension, as shown.

31 The buttstock's receiver extension channel (adjustable buttstocks only) has a keyhole profile that matches the receiver extension profile, allowing the buttstock to slide onto the receiver extension. The buttstock has a spring-loaded position stop that engages the adjustment slots in the receiver extension.

32 Pulling down on the buttstock adjustment ears or lever (depending on the model of buttstock) allows the buttstock to be moved forward or backward to achieve the desired buttstock length.

33 To install the buttstock, pull down on the buttstock adjustment lever and slide the buttstock onto the receiver extension.

34 The buttstock is now installed and can be adjusted to fit the shooter.

35 The completed lower receiver assembly.

SECTION III – UPPER RECEIVER GROUP

HEADSPACING

Prior to assembling the bolt carrier group or the upper receiver and barrel assembly, it is necessary to check the headspace of the barrel and bolt combination. The headspacing must be within safe operational tolerances before the assembled firearm can be discharged. Failure to do so could result in a catastrophic failure that may damage or render the firearm inoperable, or cause serious injury or death to the firearm operator.

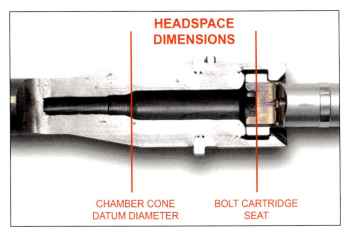

HEADSPACE DIMENSIONS

CHAMBER CONE DATUM DIAMETER   BOLT CARTRIDGE SEAT

Headspace in an AR-15 type firearm is the distance between the bolt face (the recessed area of the bolt where the base of the cartridge sits when the bolt is locked in the barrel chamber) and the datum diameter of the chamber cone (the area of the chamber that prevents the cartridge from moving forward).

Headspace dimensions are critically important to the safe operation of the AR-15 or any firearm. If headspace is less than the minimum specified, the bolt may not close properly when using the correct ammunition, causing the cartridge to jam in the chamber or causing the rifle to fire out of battery. If headspace is greater than the maximum specified, the cartridge may stretch and separate when fired, or the primer may rupture out of the cartridge. Catastrophic cartridge failures such as these could allow extremely dangerous high-pressure gas to eject fragments back toward the shooter, or damage the rifle and cause mechanical failure—all of which could lead to serious injury or death.

Headspace is measured using two precision gauges that are inserted into the rifle's chamber. One is a GO gauge, which verifies that the barrel/bolt combination provides the minimum headspace required for safe operation. The other is the NO-GO gauge, which verifies that the barrel/bolt combination provides no more than the maximum allowed headspace for safe operation. Both gauges must be used to ensure that a barrel/bolt combination will operate within safe specifications.

On a civilian application AR-15 rifle, the headspace gauge dimensions are as follows:

Headspace GO gauge dimension (minimum factory specification spacing) for a civilian AR-15 application is 1.4640 inches.

Headspace NO-GO gauge dimension (maximum factory specification spacing) for a civilian AR-15 application is 1.4670 inches.

There are two methods to check headspace— one before installing the barrel onto the upper receiver, and one after installing the barrel onto the upper receiver. It is much easier and quicker to check headspace before installing the barrel onto the upper receiver. With either method, the bolt extractor and ejector assemblies must be removed from the bolt.

It is important to reiterate that headspace must be checked for each barrel and bolt combination. Although uncommon, it is possible for one barrel to headspace correctly with one bolt and not another. Any time a bolt or a barrel is changed, the new combination must be headspaced to ensure the combination is within the safety specifications.

Because headspace must be checked with a bolt that has the extractor and ejector assemblies removed, refer to the Bolt Carrier Group Assembly section if you have a pre-assembled bolt carrier group. You can reverse the extractor and ejector assembly procedure to disassemble the bolt in order to check headspace.

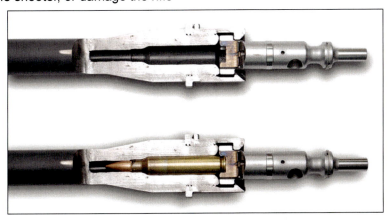

AR-15 Rifle Builder's Manual

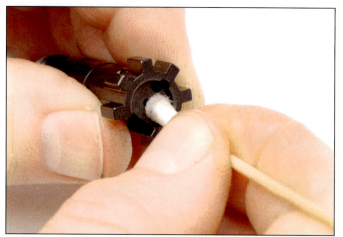

1 Use an alcohol-based solvent to clean the bolt face.

2 Use an alcohol-based solvent to clean the barrel chamber area.

3 Use an alcohol-based solvent to clean the bolt lug surfaces.

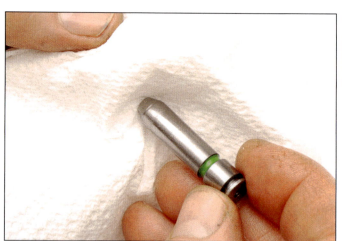

4 Use an alcohol-based solvent to clean the GO gauge surfaces.

5 Insert the GO gauge into the barrel chamber.

6 Orient the barrel as shown, with the feed ramps on the bottom and the receiver index stud at the top. Orient the bolt with the empty extractor groove aligned toward the 2 o'clock position.

7 Insert the bolt fully into the chamber and rotate the bolt clockwise. If the barrel/bolt combination meets the minimum headspace requirements, the bolt should be able to rotate closed behind the chamber lugs. If the bolt does not close on the GO gauge, the headspace is too short and the combination is UNSAFE to fire. A different bolt and/or barrel is required.

8 If the barrel/bolt combination meets the minimum headspace dimension, remove the bolt and GO gauge and insert the NO-GO gauge into the chamber.

9 Insert the bolt into the chamber as before and attempt to rotate clockwise.

10 If the barrel/bolt combination meets the maximum headspace requirement, the bolt SHOULD NOT be able to rotate closed behind the chamber lugs. If the bolt does close on the NO GO gauge and can be rotated behind the chamber lugs, the headspace exceeds the maximum headspace requirement and the combination is UNSAFE to fire. A different bolt and/or barrel is required.

Once you have confirmed that the barrel/bolt combination headspacing is within the minimum and maximum specifications, the upper receiver assembly and bolt carrier group can be assembled.

AR-15 Rifle Builder's Manual

BOLT CARRIER GROUP

Although bolt carrier groups usually come pre-assembled, headspacing a new barrel/bolt combination requires the bolt to be disassembled prior to checking the headspace. Therefore, any pre-assembled bolt must be disassembled prior to the rifle build. The disassembly process is the reverse of the following assembly process.

Bolt Carrier Group Components

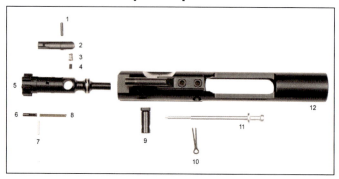

1) extractor pin, 2) extractor, 3) extractor spring, 4) extractor spring insert, 5) bolt with gas rings installed, 6) ejector, 7) ejector spring pin, 8) ejector spring, 9) cam pin, 10) firing pin retaining pin, 11) firing pin, 12) bolt carrier

Bolt Carrier Group Assembly Tools

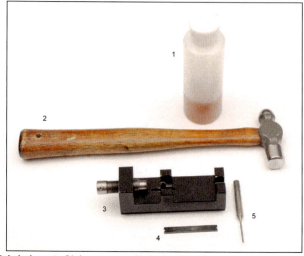

1) lubricant, 2) hammer, 3) bolt ejector tool, 4) firing pin protrusion gauge, 5) roll pin punch

FIRING PIN PROTRUSION CHECK

It is essential to check the firing pin protrusion on any new firing pin/bolt combination. On an AR-15 rifle, the firing pin must protrude a minimum of .028 inches from the bolt face and protrude no more than .036 inches when the pin is fully seated in the bolt. This is important for two reasons. First, a firing pin that does not protrude the minimum distance beyond the bolt face may not impact the primer sufficiently to ignite the primer. This will result in a failure to fire, misfire, or hang-fire condition. Second, a firing pin that protrudes more than the maximum specified distance beyond the bolt face may pierce the primer. A pierced primer is a dangerous condition that can cause damage to the firearm and injury or death to the shooter. To ensure a firing pin/bolt combination meets the specified firing pin protrusion dimensions, perform the following procedure:

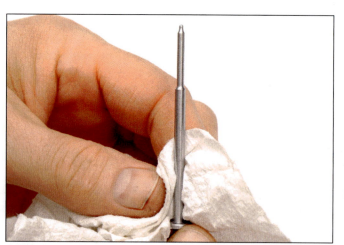

1 Thoroughly clean the firing pin with an alcohol-based solvent.

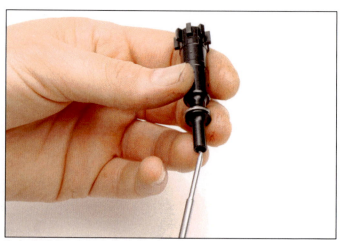

2 Insert the firing pin into the bolt as shown.

3 Press the bolt/firing pin assembly onto a flat surface so that the firing pin is fully seated against the bolt and the tip of the firing pin protrudes from the bolt face. Using the firing pin protrusion gauge end marked "MIN .028," place the gauge against the bolt face at a 90-degree angle.

4 Move the gauge so that the notch in the gauge travels over the end of the firing pin. The gauge should touch the tip of the firing pin if the firing pin protrusion meets the minimum .028 inches. If the gauge does not touch the tip of the firing pin, the firing pin is too short and a new firing pin must be acquired and similarly tested to meet the minimum specification.

5 If the firing pin protrusion meets the minimum .028-inch requirement, turn the gauge over and place the "MAX .036" end 90 degrees against the bolt face and move the gauge notch over the end of the firing pin. The gauge should not touch the tip of the firing pin. If the gauge does touch the tip of the firing pin, the firing pin is too long and a new firing pin must be acquired and similarly tested to meet the maximum specification.

BOLT CARRIER GROUP ASSEMBLY

1 Lightly lubricate the extractor spring.

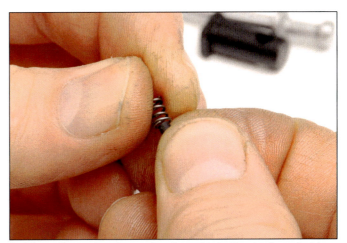

2 Place the extractor spring insert into the bottom (wide end) of the extractor spring.

3 Insert the extractor spring assembly into the extractor as shown. Push in and twist until the assembly snaps into place.

4 A correctly installed extractor spring assembly.

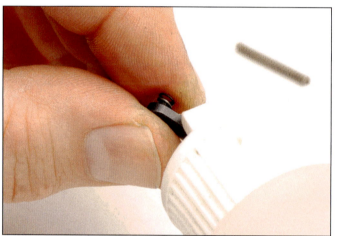

5 Lightly lubricate the extractor assembly.

6 Lightly lubricate the extractor pin.

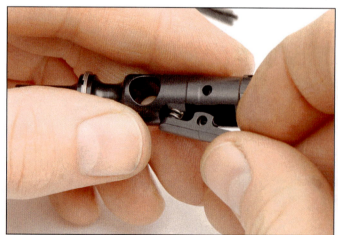

7 Position the extractor assembly into the bolt, as shown, and press firmly.

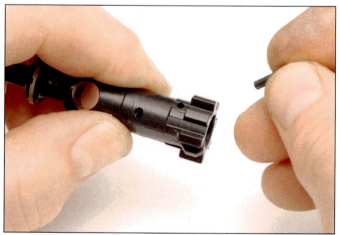

8 The extractor pivot pin holes must line up with the extractor pin holes in the bolt.

9 Insert the extractor pin into the extractor pin holes.

10 The extractor assembly correctly installed in the bolt.

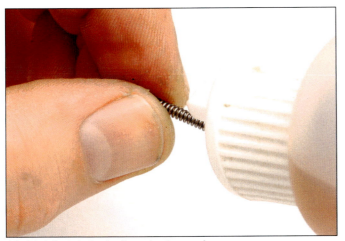
11 Lightly lubricate the ejector spring.

12 Insert the ejector spring into the ejector channel in the bolt face.

13 Lightly lubricate the ejector.

14 Position the ejector so that the slotted end is toward the bolt and the slot face is oriented toward the center of the bolt, as shown.

15 Insert the ejector partway into the ejector channel in the bolt face.

16 Position the bolt into the bolt ejector tool, as shown.

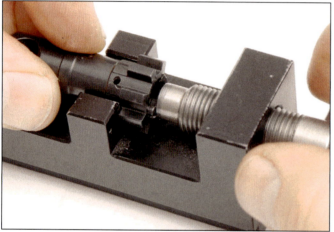

17 Compress the ejector into the bolt using the bolt ejector tool screw press. Compress the ejector into the bolt until the ejector slot clears the ejector spring pin holes in the bolt. If the ejector turned during the compression, loosen the screw press, realign the ejector, and repeat the compression process.

18 Lightly lubricate the ejector spring pin.

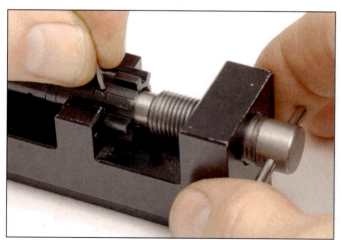

19 With the ejector slot aligned with the ejector spring pin holes, insert the ejector spring pin into the bolt.

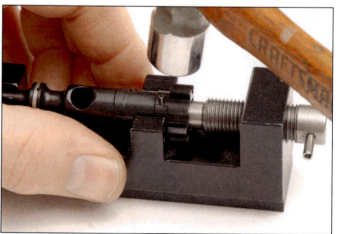

20 Start the ejector spring pin into the bolt by gently tapping it with a hammer.

21 Finish inserting the ejector spring pin into place by tapping it with a roll pin.

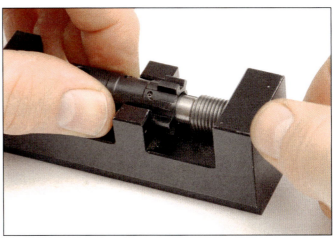

22 Be sure that both ends of the roll pin are recessed in the bolt, then remove the bolt from the press.

23 To ensure maximum gas seal around the bolt, stagger the open ends of the gas rings, as shown, by rotating them so that the open ends are not adjacent to each other.

24 Lightly lubricate the gas rings.

25 Lightly lubricate the bolt.

26 Insert the bolt into the front of the bolt carrier, as shown.

27 Rotate the bolt so that the wide side of the cam pin hole is aligned with the cam groove in the bolt carrier. Note that the cam pin will only fit into the appropriate-sized bolt cam pin hole.

28 Lightly lubricate the cam pin.

29 Insert the cam pin through the carrier and into the bolt.

30 Once inserted, rotate the cam pin 90 degrees and pull the bolt forward, as shown.

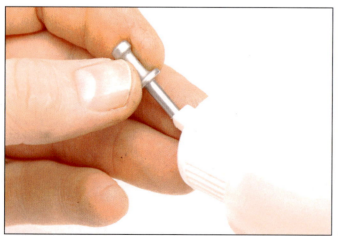

31 Lightly lubricate the firing pin.

32 Insert the firing pin tip-first into the bolt, as shown.

33 The firing pin correctly installed in the bolt.

34 Insert the firing pin retaining pin into its hole in the side of the bolt carrier, as shown.

35 With the firing pin retaining pin correctly installed, the bolt carrier group is fully assembled.

UPPER RECEIVER GROUP COMPONENTS & TOOLS

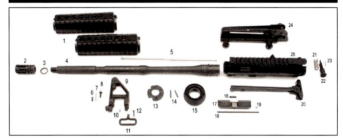

1) handguard, 2) A2 flash hider, 3) flash hider crush washer, 4) barrel, 5) gas tube, 6) front sight detent, 7) front sight detent spring, 8) front sight post, 9) front sight base, 10) gas tube pin, 11) forward sling swivel, 12) front swivel rivet, 13) handguard cap, 14) front sight base taper pins, 15) barrel nut and handguard slip ring assembly, 16) ejection port cover spring, 17) ejection port cover, 18) ejection port cover hinge pin, 19) ejection port cover hinge pin retaining ring, 20) charging handle, 21) forward assist spring, 22) forward assist plunger, 23) forward assist retainer pin, 24) detachable carry handle/rear sight assembly, 25) upper receiver

1) lubricant, 2) torque wrench, 3) GO, NO-GO gauges, 4) punch, 5) barrel nut wrench, 6) hammer, 7) upper receiver action block, 8) front sight bench block

NOTE: The following installation utilizes a stock factory barrel that does not have the front sight base pre-installed and pinned, nor has the stock factory front sight base been drilled for tapered pins. Installing and pinning a conventional MILSPEC-style front sight base to a "raw" factory barrel is a process that is best accomplished by an experienced gunsmith using proper machinery. This procedure is shown here to give the reader a complete understanding of how a MILSPEC-style barrel assembly is constructed. For ease of installation, a barrel assembly that includes the front sight base pre-installed and pinned to the barrel is recommended, or the builder can opt for an A2-style front sight base that clamps onto the barrel or secures to the barrel via set screws. Another option is to install a low-profile gas block, which is required if you wish to install a free-float handguard. Beginning with the subsection "Front Sight/Gas Tube Assembly," it will be noted where steps can be skipped when using a pre-assembled barrel and front sight base assembly.

EJECTION PORT COVER ASSEMBLY

1 The ejection port cover hinge pin retaining pin seats in this groove in the ejection port cover hinge pin.

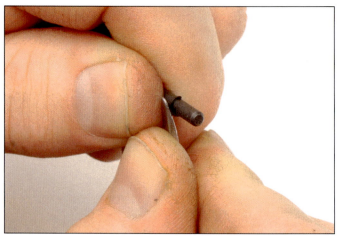

2 Insert the ejection port cover hinge pin retaining pin into the ejection port cover hinge pin groove and snap into place with a flathead screwdriver or similar tool.

3 Align the ejection port cover, as shown, between the receiver ejection port tangs and insert the ejection port cover hinge pin through the first tang and the first half of the cover.

4 Align the ejection port cover spring with the ejection port cover, as shown. The spring's long ear is oriented to the right and rests flat against the cover. Push the hinge pin through the spring far enough to secure it in place (about a third of the way).

5 When correctly installed, the ejection port cover spring is under torsional tension. This allows the port cover to open automatically when the bolt carrier is cycled through the receiver, and ensures that the port cover stays flat against the receiver when in the open position. To "load" the spring tension, the spring (short ear end, as shown) must be rotated one revolution, then the spring secured in place with the ejection port cover hinge pin. Rotate the spring so that the tension will cause the small spring ear to press against the receiver while the long spring ear presses against the ejection port cover.

6 With the ejection port cover spring rotated one revolution, hold the spring in place and push the ejection port cover hinge pin the rest of the way through the spring, port cover, and the second tang of the receiver.

7 Insert the ejection port cover hinge pin until the retaining clip seats against the receiver tang. Once the handguard cap is installed onto the barrel, the cap will prevent the pin from backing out.

8 Test the ejection port cover function. It should snap closed against the receiver and remain firmly in place.

9 When pressed from the inside (simulating the bolt carrier cycling), the cover should spring open and lay flat against the receiver.

FORWARD ASSIST ASSEMBLY

1 Lightly lubricate the forward assist plunger.

2 Lightly lubricate the forward assist spring.

3 Install the forward assist spring onto the forward assist plunger.

4 Orient the forward assist plunger and spring assembly, as shown, with the notched side facing the roll pin channel. The curved, pivoting tip of the plunger will point toward the receiver.

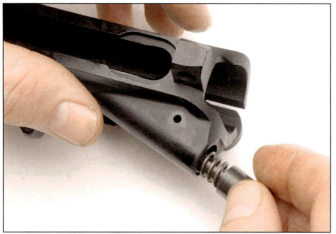

5 Insert the forward assist plunger and spring into the receiver's forward assist guide hole.

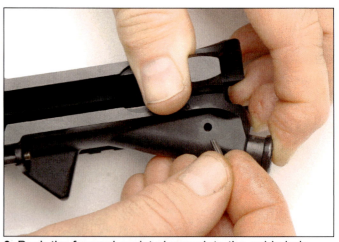

6 Push the forward assist plunger into the guide hole. The roll pin will be driven into the receiver to secure the plunger under spring tension. While the roll pin can be taped into position with the plunger depressed, some assemblers insert a small punch into the opposite side of the forward assist roll pin guide hole to keep the forward assist assembly in place, then tap the roll pin in from the opposite side, displacing the punch.

7 Whichever method is used to install the roll pin, lightly lubricate the roll pin and tap it far enough into place that it captures the forward assist plunger assembly, then stop and test the plunger action. The plunger should be able to be pushed into the guide hole, spring back when released, and remain securely in the guide hole. This indicates that the assembly is in the proper position and working correctly with no binding.

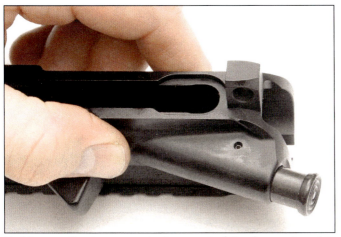

8 After confirming correct alignment of the forward assist plunger assembly, finish tapping the roll pin into place, ensuring that the ends of the roll pin are just below the receiver surface.

9 Push in and out on the forward assist plunger to ensure that it is working correctly.

FRONT SIGHT BASE/ GAS TUBE ASSEMBLY

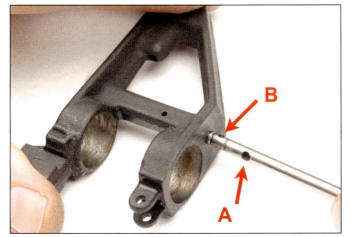

1 The gas tube is pinned to the front sight base. Note the orientation of the gas tube gas port hole (A). This port hole aligns with the gas port hole in the front sight base. The smaller hole on the forward end of the gas tube (B) accepts the gas tube pin. This hole aligns with the pin hole on the side of the front sight base. Insert the gas tube into the back of the front sight base, as shown.

2 Align the gas tube in the front sight base. The curved portion of the gas tube must be oriented upward toward the top of the front sight base in order for the tube to fit into the receiver. Line up the gas tube pin holes in the gas tube and front sight base and position the gas tube pin in the hole.

3 Use a roll pin punch to tap the gas tube pin into the front sight base.

4 The gas tube pin should seat flush with the front sight base, as shown.

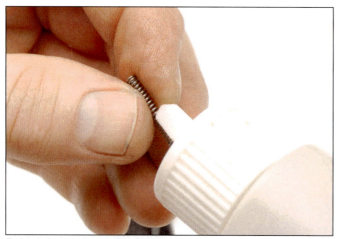

5 Lightly lubricate the front sight detent spring.

6 Insert the front sight detent spring into the front sight base, as shown.

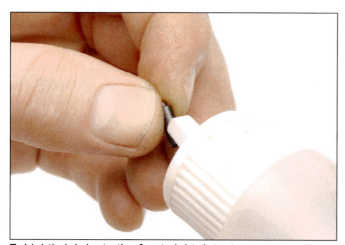

7 Lightly lubricate the front sight detent.

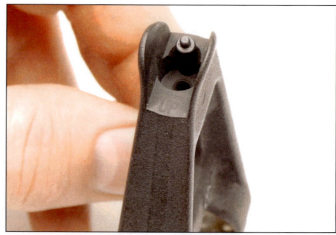

8 Insert the front sight detent onto the front sight detent spring, as shown.

9 Lightly lubricate the front sight post threads.

10 Screw the front sight post into the front sight base.

11 Once the front sight post collar contacts the front sight detent, use a flat-blade screwdriver or similar tool to depress the front sight detent enough to allow the front sight post to be screwed fully into the front sight base.

12 The front sight post properly installed. The notches in the front prevent the sight post from rotating after zero is set. To adjust the front sight post elevation, depress the front sight detent and rotate the post clockwise (up) or counterclockwise (down).

BARREL ASSEMBLY

1 Use an alcohol-based solvent to clean out the barrel chamber area.

2 Install the upper receiver securely into the upper receiver bench block and clamp the assembly into a bench vice.

3 Apply a thin coat of anti-seize lubricant to the receiver threads.

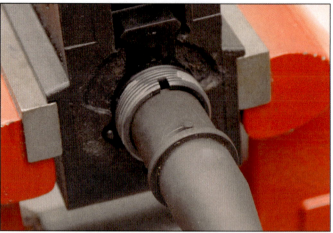

4 Align the barrel index stud (top of barrel) with the notch in the receiver and fully insert the barrel into the receiver.

5 Slide the barrel nut and handguard slip ring assembly onto the barrel.

6 Hand-tighten the assembly onto the receiver until snug.

7 Install the barrel nut wrench/torque wrench combination onto the barrel nut as shown. The barrel nut must be tightened to at least 35 lb-ft, but not to exceed 80 lb-ft. The objective is to tighten the barrel nut to at least 35 lb-ft, then tighten the nut until the next notch in the barrel nut collar aligns with the gas tube channel. The gas tube must have a clear and open channel directly to the receiver's gas tube hole.

8 Use a flat-blade screwdriver or similar tool to align the notch in the slip ring spring with the gas tube hole. This may need to be done several times during the torquing process.

9 Sighting down the barrel axis, the barrel nut/handguard slip ring assembly is correctly torqued and aligned to receive the gas tube.

IMPORTANT NOTE: The following steps are intended to illustrate the installation of a front sight base onto a "raw" barrel. These procedures should only be performed by an experienced gunsmith. When building a MILSPEC-style rifle with a front sight base, it is recommended to purchase a barrel that comes with the front sight base already drilled and pinned, or to install a clamp-on or set screw-style front sight base that does not require drilling and pinning.

When building an AR-15 rifle with an aftermarket gas block and free-float handguard, the gas block installation follows similar procedures as that of the MILSPEC-style front sight base, except aftermarket gas blocks are usually secured to the barrel via set screws or a "clamp" design and are not required to be pinned to the barrel.

10 Install the handguard cap onto the barrel as shown. The cap will stop against the barrel shoulder just behind the gas port. (NOTE: This is an exempt procedure for barrels with a pinned front sight base already installed.)

11 Slide the front sight base and gas tube assembly onto the barrel. The gas tube should insert cleanly through the barrel nut and handguard slip ring assembly and into the receiver. If there is any interference, tighten the barrel nut to the next slot in the collar, being sure not to exceed 80 lb-ft of torque. Once everything is properly aligned, the front sight base is indexed to the barrel and the assembly is ready to be drilled and pinned. (NOTE: This is an exempt procedure for barrels with a pinned front sight base already installed.)

12 To pin the front sight block to the barrel, the gunsmith/machinist ensures the front sight block is correctly indexed and secured to the barrel, and then a hole is drilled through the front sight block and a small portion of the outer barrel wall. The front sight block and barrel will then share a common pin hole. This procedure is done for both the front and the back of the sight block. (NOTE: This is an exempt procedure for barrels with a pinned front sight base already installed.)

13 A reaming tool is used to taper the pin hole in the front sight block and barrel just deep enough to allow a proper interference fit with the tapered pins. (NOTE: This is an exempt procedure for barrels with a pinned front sight base already installed.)

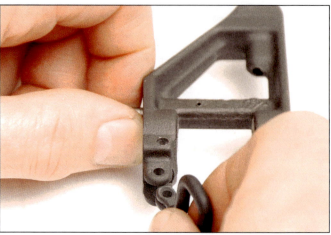

14 With the front sight block drilled for the barrel pins, the front sight block can be removed to install the sling swivel. Insert the sling swivel between the sling swivel ears of the front sight block. If your barrel included a drilled and pinned front sight base from the factory, but did not come with a pre-installed sling swivel, you can use the following procedure to install the sling swivel without removing the front sight base from the barrel.

15 Insert the sling swivel rivet through the front sight base and sling swivel.

16 Position the rivet in a rivet press and expand the end of the rivet until the sling swivel is secured.

17 Install the front sight block and gas tube assembly onto the barrel. (NOTE: This is an exempt procedure for barrels with a pinned front sight base already installed.)

18 Remove the upper receiver assembly from the vice block and position the front sight base onto a front sight block with the "PINS IN" text on top, as shown. (NOTE: This is an exempt procedure for barrels with a pinned front sight base already installed.)

AR-15 Rifle Builder's Manual

19 Carefully align the front sight block pin holes with the barrel pin holes and insert the tapered pin. (NOTE: This is an exempt procedure for barrels with a pinned front sight base already installed.)

20 Tap the pin partially into the front sight block. (NOTE: This is an exempt procedure for barrels with a pinned front sight base already installed.)

21 Use a punch and hammer to fully seat the pin into the front sight base. (NOTE: This is an exempt procedure for barrels with a pinned front sight base already installed.)

22 Repeat for the remaining pin. (NOTE: This is an exempt procedure for barrels with a pinned front sight base already installed.)

FLASH HIDER ASSEMBLY

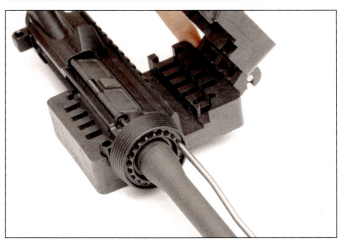

1 Fit the upper receiver assembly into the upper receiver vice block and clamp into the bench vice.

2 Install the flash hider crush washer onto the barrel with the cupped face pointing toward the muzzle.

AR-15 Rifle Builder's Manual

3 Apply a light coat of anti-seize lubricant to the muzzle threads.

4 Screw the flash hider finger-tight onto the barrel.

5 The A2 flash hider has a flat portion on one side that must be pointed downward (6 o'clock position) when properly installed. This is to prevent muzzle blast from blowing dirt and debris when shooting close to the ground, as in a prone position. When using a crush washer, the flash hider does not need to be torqued to a specific number. Once the flash hider is installed hand tight, use an armorer wrench or similar tool to rotate the flash hider until the flat portion is at the 6 o'clock position (seen here). The minimum rotation after hand tightening should be no less than 90 degrees and no more than 460 degrees.

CHARGING HANDLE & BOLT CARRIER GROUP INSTALLATION

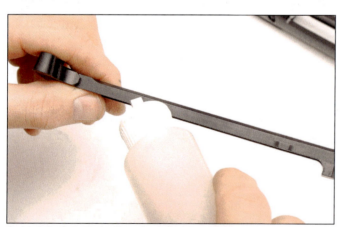

1 Lightly lubricate the charging handle.

2 Turn the upper receiver assembly upside down and install the charging handle upside down, as shown. The charging handle fits into the charging handle channel at the top of the receiver. Slide the charging handle along the channel until it falls into place.

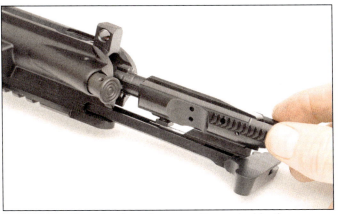 

3 With the charging handle correctly seated in the receiver, the bolt carrier group can now be inserted into the receiver. Pull the bolt as far out of the carrier as it will go, then install the bolt upside down, with the gas key seated in the bottom of the charging handle, as shown.

4 Push the bolt carrier group into the receiver. As you do so, the gas key will push the charging handling along with it. Push in until the charging handle locks into the receiver.

5 The bolt carrier group and charging handle are now properly installed in the receiver.

CARRY HANDLE/REAR SIGHT ASSEMBLY

1 With the carry handle/rear sight assembly clamping screws loosened, place the assembly over top of the upper receiver Picatinny rail, as shown. Align the assembly so that the front of the carry handle is in line with the front of the rail.

2 Tighten the clamping screws hand-tight to complete the installation.

HANDGUARD INSTALLATION

 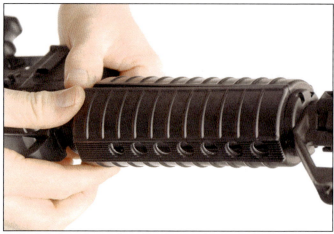

1 Place the back of the upper receiver assembly on a bench top or suitably sturdy surface. With one hand, pull down on the handguard slip ring. With the other hand, insert the front (small tapered end) of the lower half of the handguard into the handguard cap and the rear (large end) of the lower handguard into the slip ring.

2 Switch hands on the slip ring and repeat for the upper half of the hand guard installation.

AR-15 Rifle Builder's Manual

SECTION IV – UPPER/LOWER RECEIVER ASSEMBLY & FUNCTION CHECK

UPPER & LOWER RECEIVER GROUP ASSEMBLY

1 Ensure that the hammer is in the cocked position and mate the upper and lower receivers at the pivot pin holes. Once aligned, push the pivot pin through the holes until it clicks into place.

2 Align the takedown pin holes and push the takedown pin through the holes until it clicks into place. The rifle is now fully assembled and ready for the function check.

FUNCTION CHECK

The purpose of a function check is to ensure that the trigger assembly and the fire control selector work correctly. A function check should be performed not only at the completion of a rifle build, but any time the upper and lower receivers are disconnected at the takedown pin, or are completely separated during routine maintenance or repair. When performing a function check:

- make sure that the muzzle is pointed in a safe direction
- make sure there is no magazine in the magazine well
- make sure you have visually and physically checked the chamber to ensure there are no obstructions in the receiver and there are no live rounds of ammunition in the rifle

1 Pull back on the charging handle and release.

2 Place the fire control selector in the FIRE position.

3 Pull back on the trigger and HOLD. Do not let up on the trigger. The hammer should have released ("dry-fired").

4 While keeping the trigger pulled all the way back, pull all the way back on the charging handle and release the charging handle while continuing to keep the trigger pulled back.

5 Slowly let up on the trigger, allowing the trigger to move forward. You will feel and hear a "click" as the trigger resets.

6 Pull back on the trigger. The hammer should have released ("dry-fired").

7 Remove your finger from the trigger and pull back on the charging handle and release.

8 Rotate the fire control selector to the SAFE position.

9 Pull back on the trigger. The trigger should not move backwards and the hammer should not release.

10 Rotate the fire control selector to the FIRE position and pull back on the trigger. The hammer should have released ("dry-fired").

If the function check performed as described, the trigger and safety selector assemblies are in safe working order. If the function check did not perform as described, examine the trigger assembly and safety selector to determine what is causing the malfunction and correct the issue.

SECTION V – AR-15 OPERATION

Safe firearm handling is the foundation of firearms operation. As a firearms owner or controller, it is your responsibility to ensure that your firearm is handled and operated in a safe manner and is under your control at all times. Always follow these basic safe handling procedures any time you are in possession of or are operating a firearm.

1. Always treat a firearm as if it has a cartridge in the chamber and is ready to fire.
2. Always keep the muzzle pointed in a safe direction, and always keep your finger off the trigger until you are ready to shoot.
3. Always ensure that the fire control selector is in the SAFE position until you are ready to pull the trigger and shoot.
4. Never load or charge (place a cartridge into the chamber) before you are ready to shoot at a safe target.
5. When in a shooting range environment and you are not on the firing line, ensure that fire control selector is on SAFE, the magazine is removed from the rifle, the bolt is in the open position, and there is no cartridge in the chamber or the receiver. This shows you and those around you that the firearm is rendered safe.
6. Always shoot the firearm in a safe direction and into a backstop that will stop the bullet and prevent the bullet from ricocheting.
7. Always be sure that the area downrange of your target is free of people, structure, vehicles, animals, or other potential safety hazards.
8. Always wear approved safety glasses and ear protection when shooting a firearm.
9. Always keep your firearm stored in a safe location that only you have access to.
10. Prior to shooting your firearm, perform a function check to ensure the firearm's trigger assembly and fire control selector are working properly. (Refer to the Function Check section under Group Assembly & Function Check for the process of checking function.)

MAGAZINE LOADING

1 Firmly grip the magazine as shown.

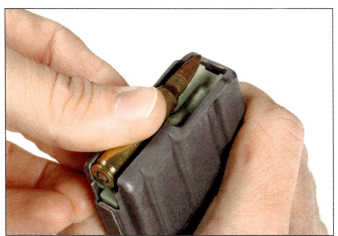

2 With your other hand, place a cartridge on top of the magazine follower and push down on the cartridge.

3 Place the next cartridge on top of the first and push down.

4 Continue loading the magazine to the desired capacity or until you reach the capacity of the magazine. A standard 5.56mm magazine holds 30 rounds.

LOADING & DISCHARGING

1 Before loading your firearm, be sure the fire control selector is on SAFE and there is no magazine in the magazine well.

2 Pull back on the charging handle and push in on the bottom of the bolt stop to hold the bolt in the open position.

3 Inspect the receiver and chamber both visually and with your finger to ensure there is no cartridge present.

4 Insert a loaded magazine into the magazine well, pushing the magazine up into the magazine well until it clicks into place.

AR-15 Rifle Builder's Manual

5 Pull all the way back on the charging handle until it stops.

6 Release the charging handle while the charging handle is in the rearward position, allowing the bolt to move forward under spring tension. The bolt will strip a cartridge from the magazine and seat it in the chamber. Be sure not to "ride" the bolt forward by maintaining a grip on the charging handle.

7 An alternative to pulling back and releasing the charging handle when the bolt is in the open locked position is to press the top of the bolt stop. Depressing the bolt stop will release the bolt and allow it to travel forward and chamber a cartridge.

8 When you are on target and ready to shoot, use your thumb to move the fire selector switch from SAFE to FIRE. The firearm is now "hot" and ready to fire. To fire the weapon, pull back on the trigger.

AR-15 CYCLE OF OPERATION

The AR-15 is a semi-automatic rifle, which means the system is designed to eject the empty cartridge, recock the hammer, and chamber a new cartridge automatically. The rifle cannot fire again until the operator releases the trigger enough for it to reset. This is called the cycle of operation. There are eight steps in the cycle of operation:

1. **Firing** - Pulling back the trigger releases the hammer, which strikes the firing pin. The firing pin impacts the cartridge primer and ignites the powder charge. As the expanding gas pushes the bullet down the barrel, some of the gas exits the barrel through the gas block and travels down the gas tube. This gas pushes against the gas key on top of the bolt carrier.

2. **Unlocking** - As the bolt begins to move rearward by the gas, the bolt cam pin rotates the bolt so that the bolt disengages, or unlocks, from the chamber lugs.

3. **Extracting** - Once the bolt is unlocked from the chamber lugs, the bolt carrier continues to travel backwards, with the bolt extracting the empty cartridge from the chamber.

4. **Ejecting** - As the bolt carrier group moves rearward and clears the ejection port, the bolt's ejector and extractor work together to "flip" the empty cartridge

AR-15 CYCLE OF OPERATION (continued)

out through the ejection port.

5. **Cocking** - While the bolt carrier moves rearward, it rides across the hammer, recocking it.

6. **Feeding** - Once the bolt carrier group has expended all energy created by the gas, the action spring pushes the bolt carrier group forward. As the bolt travels forward, it strips the next available cartridge from the magazine and pushes it towards the chamber.

7. **Chambering** - The forward motion of the bolt pushes the cartridge into the chamber.

8. **Locking** - As the bolt carrier continues to move forward, the bolt cam pin rotates the bolt behind the chamber lugs, locking the bolt into place. Once the shooter lets up on the trigger and the trigger resets, the rifle is ready to fire again and the cycle of operation repeats with the next round fired.

9 When the last round has been fired (magazine empty), the bolt will catch on the bolt stop as it moves forward.

10 Move the fire control selector to the SAFE position.

11 Depress the magazine release button and remove the empty magazine from the magazine well.

UNLOADING & MAKING SAFE

An AR-15's cycle of operation ensures that a live, unfired cartridge is always in the chamber until all rounds in a magazine have been fired. Because of this, there are several steps involved in order to render the firearm safe should you discontinue firing before emptying a magazine.

1 When you discontinue firing the rifle while live rounds remain in the magazine, place your finger outside of the trigger guard and move the fire selector to the SAFE position. REMEMBER, there is a live round in the chamber.

2 While keeping the firearm pointed in a safe direction, depress the magazine release button and remove the magazine.

3 Pull rearward on the charging handle while observing the ejection port. Visually observe the live round as it ejects through the ejection port.

4 Visually, and with your finger, inspect the chamber and receiver to ensure there are no live rounds present. Because the magazine is out of the magazine well, you must lock the bolt open by depressing the bolt lock while the charging handle is pulled back.

5 Once you have verified that the chamber is empty and there are no live rounds in the receiver, pull back on the charging handle to unlock the bolt and then allow the bolt to move to its forward and locked position. Snap the ejection port cover closed for storage.

ZEROING & MARKSMANSHIP

The A2-style rear sight and the A2-style front sight base combination shown here are both adjustable. The rear sight is adjustable for windage and elevation, while the front sight is adjustable for elevation only. This sighting system allows the operator to zero the rifle with what is commonly referred to as a "combat" or "battle" zero.

The theory behind the battle zero is that it makes use of the 5.56mm NATO round's ballistics to deliver a lethal point-of-impact across a wide distance. The U.S. Army standard is a 25/300 meter battle zero. In theory, a rifle that is zeroed at 25 meters will have similar point-of-impact at 300 meters, and the trajectory of the bullet between these two distances will keep the point-of-impact within the vitals zone of a human-sized target. As a result, one sight setting can allow a soldier to lethally engage targets from point-blank range to 300 meters without the need for sight adjustment.

1. Adjusting the front sight elevation with a front sight adjustment tool.
2. Adjusting the rear sight windage.
3. Adjusting the rear sight elevation.
4. Selecting between the short-range (large) and long-range (small) aperture.

The A2-style rear sight shown here has an elevation knob that, once the rifle has been fine-tuned for a 300-meter zero, delivers zero at the ranges beyond 300 meters as indicated on the elevation knob. The U.S. Army and U.S. Marine Corps apply two different standards for battle zero, and it is suggested that the reader examine both standards to determine which best suits their need. These standards are detailed in the U.S. Army Field Manual FM 3-22.9 and the U.S. Marine Corps manual MCRP 3-01A.

In addition to providing valuable information on the M16/M4 weapon systems, of which the AR-15 rifle is a derivative, these manuals cover a broad range of operational and marksmanship instruction of use to veteran and novice AR-15 shooters alike. Refer to these manuals for specific details on sighting in and the practical use of your AR-15 rifle.

Army Field Manual FM 3-22.9, Rifle Marksmanship M16/M4-Series Weapons (http://www.globalsecurity.org/military/library/policy/army/fm/3-22-9/fm3-22-9_c1_2011.pdf)

Marine Corps Rifle Marksmanship manual MCRP 3-01A (https://archive.org/stream/MCRP3-01A#page/n0/mode/2up)

SECTION VI – SERVICE & LUBRICATION

As with any firearm, routine inspection and cleaning will ensure long life and reliable operation of your rifle. As such, it is recommended that the AR-15 be cleaned following each shooting session and prior to storage. Dutiful and thorough cleaning and lubrication will not only help mitigate malfunctions, but will also prevent carbon and fouling build up on critical components that could cause malfunctions or component failure.

Every AR-15 owner should have a comprehensive cleaning kit. This includes items and supplies to clean the barrel bore, chamber, and bolt carrier group. One of the most complete kits on the market today is the MSR/AR Cleaning System from Otis Technology. With this kit, along with disposable items such as cleaning patches and a supply of Cleaner-Lubricant-Protectant (CLP), you have everything necessary to perform regular cleaning and lubrication of your AR-15 rifle.

RIFLE CLEANING & LUBRICATION

1 General cleaning of the AR-15 involves separation of the upper and lower receiver assemblies, as well as separating the bolt and bolt carrier. Periodically, it is recommended that you remove the buffer and action spring assembly for cleaning and lubrication, and disassemble the extractor from the bolt to give the bolt assembly a thorough cleaning and lubrication. For general cleaning and lubrication, however, the disassembly shown here is sufficient when shooting under normal range conditions.

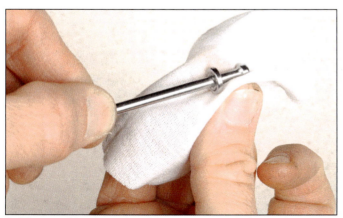

2 Thoroughly clean the firing pin, especially the flat shoulder on the pin side. Excessive carbon buildup here can affect firing pin protrusion.

3 A clean cam pin will ensure smooth rotation of the bolt in the bolt carrier.

4 The firing pin retaining pin should be kept clean, as it is an easy "catch" for carbon fouling.

5 The bolt is the most time-consuming portion of the bolt carrier assembly to clean due to the varied surface angles.

6 The Otis Technology BONE tool can help scrape heavy fouling from the back of the bolt, as seen here, as well as the firing pin shoulder and the inside of the bolt carrier.

7 Here is the BONE tool scraping carbon from inside the bolt carrier. It is not a necessary tool, but a helpful one when you encounter stubborn fouling.

8 Remove fouling from both the exterior and the interior surfaces of the bolt carrier. Occasionally, use a pipe cleaner or a worn, suitably sized bore brush to clean the gas key.

9 Although it doesn't receive heavy build-up, the charging handle should be cleaned regularly.

10 A chamber brush is needed to clean out the chamber.

11 Another tool by Otis that works well for scraping fouling from behind the chamber lugs is their "Star Chamber" scraper. Simply insert past the chamber lugs and rotate.

12 Cord-style bore cleaners (bore snakes) are the most convenient tool for cleaning a rifle barrel. The combination of cloth fibers and embedded or screw-on brushes do an effective job of removing fouling with one or two pull-throughs. These are ideal for routine maintenance. Follow the cleaner/solvent/lubricant manufacturer's recommendations for exact barrel cleaning procedures for the products you are using.

13 Dirt and fouling can work their way into the receiver. When cleaning the receiver, only use nylon brushes, as metal brushes can damage the aluminum receiver.

Prior to assembly, it is recommended to LIGHTLY coat the parts disassembled for cleaning with CLP. DO NOT over-lubricate, as this can hold dust and debris and create function problems. The following components can be lubricated with CLP applied lightly with your finger:
- Bolt carrier rails
- Gas rings
- Exterior of the bolt and bolt lugs
- Bolt cam pin
- Takedown and pivot pins
- Hammer face

The following components should receive a single drop of lubricant:
- Forward assist
- Dust cover pin
- Bolt catch
- Magazine catch
- Hammer and trigger pins
- Ejector (allow to seep into pocket)
- Rear sight
- Front sight post and detent

Occasionally, it is recommended to remove the buffer and action spring assembly to clean and lightly lubricate. A dry or dirty buffer spring can interfere with the rifle's cycle of operation. To remove the buffer spring from the receiver extension, depress the buffer retainer and slowly let out the spring tension as you guide the spring/buffer out of the receiver extension. This is under pressure, so be sure to maintain control of the spring as you remove it.

MAGAZINE SERVICE

Magazines for AR-15 style rifles are designed so that they can be disassembled for cleaning. A dirty magazine can cause a failure to feed condition, or prevent the magazine from properly locking into the receiver. Standard 30-round steel magazines are easy to service. Service involves disassembling the magazine, removing dirt and debris from the magazine and spring, and lightly lubricating the spring.

1 Insert an appropriate tool into the hole in the floorplate and simultaneously pry upward and push the floorplate forward, as shown.

2 Notice that the floorplate retains the spring under tension. Place your finger over the spring as you slide the floorplate out of the base of the magazine.

3 Pull the spring out of the magazine.

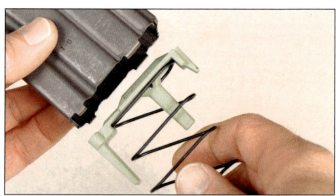

4 Manipulate the follower until it becomes free of the magazine.

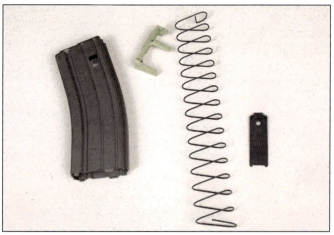

5 Once disassembled, the magazine assembly can be cleaned, lightly lubricated, and then reassembled in the reverse order of disassembly.

SECTION VII – TROUBLESHOOTING

The following is taken from U.S. Army Operator's Manual TM9-1005-319-10 and TM 9-1005-319-23&P

FAILURE TO FIRE

- **Check for:** Selector lever on SAFE; **Action:** Place selector on FIRE
- **Check for:** Improper assembly of firing pin; **Action:** Retaining pin goes in back of large shoulder of firing pin
- **Check for:** Broken or chipped firing pin; **Action:** [Replace]
- **Check for:** Too much oil in firing pin recess; **Action:** Wipe out with pipe cleaner
- **Check for:** Defective ammo; **Action:** Remove and discard
- **Check for:** Too much carbon on firing pin or in firing pin recess; **Action:** Clean
- **Check for:** Firing mechanism and/or lower receiver assembly improperly assembled or has worn, broken, or missing parts; **Action:** [Inspect for problem and replace/repair as necessary]
- **Check for:** Broken, defective, or missing firing pin retaining pin; **Action:** [Replace]
- **Check for:** Selector lever frozen on SAFE position; **Action:** [see Selector Lever Binds]

FAILURE TO LOCK

- **Check for:** Bolt cam pin missing; **Action:** [Replace]
- **Check for:** Loose or damaged bolt carrier key; **Action:** [Inspect and repair or replace]
- **Check for:** Improperly assembled extractor spring assembly; **Action:** Assemble correctly
- **Check for:** Bent gas tube; **Action:** Adjust to its original configuration by bending in the area of the handguard assembly. If the gas tube cannot be returned to its original configuration, [disassemble and replace].
- **Check for:** Weak or broken action spring; **Action:** Replace action spring

FAILURE TO UNLOCK

- **Check for:** Dirty or burred locking lugs on bolt; **Action:** [Clean bolt. If burred, remove burrs or replace with new bolt, being sure to headspace the new bolt.]
- **Check for:** Burred lugs on barrel extension; **Action:** Remove burrs
- **Check for:** Short recoil; **Action:** [See Short Recoil]

FAILURE TO EXTRACT

- **Check for:** Broken extractor spring; **Action:** [Inspect extractor spring and replace if necessary.]
- **Check for:** Frozen extractor; **Action:** Remove and clean
- **Check for:** Dirty or corroded ammo; **Action:** Remove. Push out stuck round with cleaning rod
- **Check for:** Carbon in chamber; **Action:** Clean chamber
- **Check for:** Fouling or carbon in extractor recess or lip; **Action:** Clean
- **Check for:** Short recoil; **Action:** [See Short Recoil]
- **Check for:** Restricted buffer assembly; **Action:** Remove and clean
- **Check for:** Restricted movement of bolt carrier group; **Action:** Remove, clean, and lubricate. Before putting bolt back in, make sure gas tube fits into carrier key and that the carrier moves freely.

FAILURE TO EJECT

- **Check for:** Broken cartridge ejector; **Action:** Replace
- **Check for:** Cartridge ejector stuck in bolt body; **Action:** Disassemble and clean
- **Check for:** Weak or broken ejector spring; **Action:** replace
- **Check for:** Short recoil; **Action:** [See Short Recoil]

FAILURE OF MAGAZINE TO LOCK IN RIFLE

- Check for: Dirty or corroded magazine catch; Action: Disassemble and clean
- Check for: Defective magazine catch spring; Action: [Disassemble and replace]
- Check for: Worn or broken magazine catch; Action: [Disassemble and replace]

FAILURE TO FEED

- **Check for:** Dirty or corroded ammo; **Action:** Clean
- **Check for:** Dirty magazine; **Action:** Clean
- **Check for:** Defective magazine; **Action:** Replace
- **Check for:** Too many rounds in magazine; **Action:** Take out excess
- **Check for:** Action of buffer assembly is restricted; **Action:** Take out buffer and spring and clean
- **Check for:** Magazine catch spring weak or broken; **Action:** [Disassemble and replace]
- **Check for:** Magazine catch defective; **Action:** [Disassemble and replace]
- **Check for:** Magazine not fully seated; **Action:** Adjust magazine catch [by pressing in on the magazine release button on the right side and rotating the magazine catch on the left side either clockwise to tighten or counterclockwise to loosen]
- **Check for:** Short recoil; **Action:** [See Short Recoil]

DOUBLE FEED

- **Check for:** Defective magazine; **Action:** Replace

FAILURE TO CHAMBER

- **Check for:** Dirty or corroded ammo; **Action:** Clean
- **Check for:** Damaged ammo; **Action:** Replace
- **Check for:** Carbon in chamber or on gas tube; **Action:** Clean
- **Check for:** Dirt, corrosion, or carbon buildup in barrel locking lugs; **Action:** Clean lugs
- **Check for:** Weak or broken action spring; Action: Replace
- **Check for:** Short recoil; **Action:** [See Short Recoil]

FAILURE TO COCK

- **Check for:** Worn, broken, or missing parts of firing mechanism; **Action:** [Inspect, repair, and/or replace defective components]
- **Check for:** Short recoil; **Action:** [See Short Recoil]

SHORT RECOIL

- **Check for:** Gaps in bolt rings (not staggered); **Action:** Stagger ring gaps
- **Check for:** Carbon or dirt in carrier key or on outside of gas tube; **Action:** Clean
- **Check for:** Q-Tip/pipe cleaner stuck inside carrier key; **Action:** [Remove obstruction]
- **Check for:** Broke or damaged action spring; **Action:** Replace
- **Check for:** Unlubricated or dirty action spring and receiver extension; **Action:** Clean and lubricate
- **Check for:** Gas leakage caused by broken or loose gas tube; **Action:** [Inspect, repair, and/or replace defective components.]

BOLT FAILS TO LOCK TO REAR AFTER LAST ROUND

- **Check for:** Dirty or corroded bolt latch; **Action:** Clean
- **Check for:** Magazine follower worn or broken; **Action:** Replace magazine
- **Check for:** Magazine catch spring weak or broken; **Action:** Replace magazine
- **Check for:** Magazine feeder lips bent or broken; **Action:** Replace magazine
- **Check for:** Broken bolt catch and/or spring; **Action:** Replace

SELECTOR LEVER BINDS

- **Check for:** Faulty magazine; **Action:** Replace
- **Check for:** Needs oil; **Action:** Lubricate with CLP
- **Check for:** Dirt or sand under trigger; **Action:** Clean

BOLT CARRIER "HANG-UP"

- **Check for:** Round jammed between bolt and charging handle and/or double-feed; **Action:** KEEP CLEAR OF MUZZLE and 1) remove magazine 2) push in on the bottom of the bolt latch, and 3) bang rifle butt on the ground while pulling back on charging handle. Bolt should lock to the rear. 4) While bolt is held to the rear, the round should fall through the magazine well. If this procedure fails, use a section of cleaning rod to push the bolt fully to the rear through the ejection port.

NOTES

Made in the USA
Monee, IL
30 December 2020